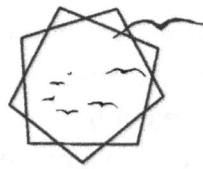

REVIEWS

"Matthew Crowley explores the edges of the material and the ephemeral, traveling by means of gratitude and questioning between physical expanses and the equal vastness of an interior world. It is into this luminous inner space that the poet's sometimes sure, sometimes trembling hand makes an especially compelling guide."

—Gussie Fauntleroy, award-winning journalist, writer, editor, and poet.

"To openly engage the world is no easy task. It is easy to retire into that which is certain, comfortable, and easily navigated. Matthew Crowley is an adventurous seeker who avoids the spiritual interstate and chooses instead to ride a long and meandering road into the edge lands. In this book, we follow him down inward two-lanes that can't be googled. And we join him on byways that lead us into unfathomable and limitless wildness. This book is a generous and honest sharing of the conundrums and the wonders he has lived along the way."

—Peter Anderson, author *First Church of the Higher Elevations*

"The feelings are deep and beautiful. There are lots of tears, as happens in life. Lots of golden light. In Farsi, where Matthew Crowley draws his inspiration, poetry seems inseparable from the sacred. As it does here, each poem a hymn to the restlessness of a spirit feeling its way into the mystery."

—Art Goodtimes

"Matthew Crowley often brightens up Crestone gatherings—performances, ceremonies, parties—with his flawlessly recited poetry, and now it is published. His voice comes through the print. These are poems to be read aloud.

"Here is half a lifetime (more to come) of writing that is both expressive and lyrical, as reflected even in the title, "Limitlessness," a word with a denotation that might ring a bell in any of the spiritual compounds around here and a sound like wind gusting up from our sandy San Luis Valley to the high Sangre de Cristo mountains.

"Perhaps owing to his job as community liaison for the Shumei International Institute, his poems have a Shinto quality, but they are not fake copies of Japanese poetry. Matthew is not a parrot. And owing to his life of hard work, communication and, now, fatherhood, his poems are accessible and unpretentious. Matthew is not a peacock. On the contrary, as you will discover, there is a crow in his name."

—Larry Joseph Calloway, Journalist with a recent MA in Eastern Classics, St. John's College of Santa Fe

Matthew P. Crowley
CrowsOutpost.com

LIMITLESSNESS

LIMITLESSNESS

a collection of poems

MATTHEW P. CROWLEY

Limitlessness: a collection of poems
Copyright ©2014 Matthew P. Crowley

ISBN: 978-1-940769-26-4
Publisher: Mercury HeartLink
Printed in the United States of America

Back cover photo by Lori Nagel and Sunflower Studios.

Contact the author at: www.crowsoutpost.com

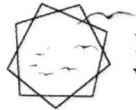

Mercury HeartLink
www.heartlink.com

LIMITLESSNESS

ONE

Two

THREE

FOUR

List of Illustrations

Marika Popovits

Cover image — *The Holy Fire of God's Alchemical Gold*

Marika Popovits' most recent series of eight watercolors titled "Golden Overmind", maintains the flow of an unfolding manifestation of Creation, both energetically and formally. It refers to a specific domain in consciousness which in various cultures has been defined symbolically as the "realm of the gods". The cover image from that series is used here with the artist's gracious permission.

Matthew P. Crowley

Photographs by the author capture three of his primary interests, the intersection of the spiritual and material worlds, earth magick and barefoot in The Muddly Puddle family fun. These photos were taken in his neighborhood, the uniquely beautiful ecosystem and spiritually diverse cultural landscape of the Crestone, Colorado area. They have been rendered here in grayscale.

Acknowledgements

I'd like to express gratitude to everyone I've ever met and everything I've ever experienced; all of the good and all of the so called "bad", without which and whom—I would not be exactly who and what it seems I am. A little more specifically... I want to thank James O'Dea who's subtle alchemical magick in appointing himself my 'Writer's Conscience' was just the gentle push that was needed at just the right time. Gratitude for the *multitude* of writers and poets who have gone before me, inspiring me. To Mercury HeartLink and Stewart S. Warren who's own poetic proliferation continues to inspire and whose wisdom in things print and technical put these words in book form and on line.

I would also like to thank my friends Peter Anderson, Larry Calloway, Marv Mattis, Michael Hayes, Paul Winter, Reggie Ray, Terry Goergen, Gussie Fauntleroy, Art Goodtimes and Marika Popovits who found time in their lives to read draft manuscripts of this book and offer their support, criticism and suggestions in bringing it to light. Gratitude to Marika Popovits also for her gracious permission to use her extraordinary visual art to accompany my word art in this collection. For my brother Paul for our lifelong teaching/ learning relationship and for leaving poetry on my voice mail, showing me 'I could too'. And to all my Crow ancestors and relatives particularly my mother Anna Cecile Crowley who taught me the secrets of the night and to Tammy, Danny, Morgan and Thom to whom the Word speaks.

And especially for the unwavering support of my beloved Kelly and Arthur without whom I might never have experienced the "...trinity of love by morning's light."

HEARTDRIVE

It began with a voice mail, my brother Paul sharing a contemporary poem[1] inspired by an ancient one in Farsi. Out of love and repetition I listened to it again and again, and without intending to realized I had nearly remembered that poem by heart. Just one last intentional effort and it was fully *downloaded into my heartdrive*. Years later I would learn that Hafiz, the original Sufi author of that ancient Farsi poem, was not a name but rather a title (Hafez) given to those who had "remembered" the entire Koran by heart. I am grateful to that which taught me—"You don't memorize poetry, you *remember it by heart*."

I can't explain precisely just what it is... Some poems simply cry out to be heard, not read; Rumi – "A Cap to Wear in Both Worlds", Hafiz – "Forgive the Dream", Pablo Neruda – "This is Where We Live", Mary Oliver – "Ghosts", Adyashanti – "Smoke Over Fire". I encounter them, hear them or read them once and my heart sings out for me to download them into my heartdrive so they might be sung back to others who also thirst for this wine.

The great Sufi mystics like Rumi and Hafiz, never wrote down their own poems. Fortunately for us, there were "those with ears to hear" who followed them around scribbling, at times I imagine furiously, in an attempt to 'capture' the words that flew spontaneously from *their* hearts. It is my profound belief that many poems are better heard than read. For this reason I have decided to also make audio recordings of poems in this collection available to those who might like to listen to some as well as read them. If you too 'have ears to hear' and a longing to do so, visit my website at *www.CrowsOutpost.com* where you can listen to and download audio files of selected poems free of charge, and to see a calendar of recitations and related events.

1. *I Can See Angels* – Poems by Hafiz, Translations by Daniel Ladinsky

INTRODUCTION

My spiritual practice has taught me that words are merely "symbols of symbols." So much potential for confusion, misunderstanding and, now and again, that something else. I find a paradoxical 'forgetting of the words' when I remove them from the page, *'download them to my heartdrive'*. There are the symbols of the characters—letters, words. There are definitions of those words. There is what those words mean to *you*, me, others. There are emotions and memories evoked by certain words and phrases which are slightly or completely different for each one of us. Then, when we give voice to them, there are sounds associated with these words—vibrations, notes, frequencies and rhythms within these sounds.

I didn't have a word for this until I first heard the Japanese word "*kototama*" (sometimes spelled *kotodama*). This word literally translates as "word spirit". (*Koto* "word/speech" and *tama* or *dama* "spirit/soul"). As I was taught, *kototama* was the underlying reason we (A Japanese based spiritual community known as Shumei) were chanting a 3,000 year old Shinto prayer in Japanese language so archaic that even my Japanese friends could not understand most of the meaning of the words. I was told "It's not the meaning of the words but more the vibration, the sound and *spirit* of the words that matters." Something lit up in me in that moment, a deepening explanation and consciousness for why I was doing what I had already been doing for years.

Most often it is the so called "meaning" of a poem that first attracts me to download it to my heartdrive. Once it's firmly installed and I can give voice to it in the highly particular way I hear it being spoken, I find I have become equally interested in the way it sounds as I am in what it might "mean". It becomes for me a song. I have reflected long upon the *process* of downloading poetry into my heartdrive. What happens to us when, through repetition, commitment, love... we take the symbols off the page and put them in our hearts? What magick can we conjure by calling up these verses in those *'just right'* moments when a segue arises? What effect does it have on our own voice as writers to download the words of the great masters into our being?

I like to encourage people listening to or reading poetry to forget what the poet meant when they wrote the poem—don't even try. Rather, see what it means to you at that moment. What feelings, memories, thoughts does the poem evoke? Billy Collins, past national poet laureate and professor of English speaks well of this in his poem "Introduction to Poetry", when he says "But all they want to do is tie it to a chair and torture a confession out of it." Of course there is nothing wrong with loving a poem intellectually, emotionally or for any other reason. I think there are as many reasons to love a poem as there are individuals in this world. I simply encourage all of us to see what arises from within ourselves first.

Some esoteric information regarding kototama was shared with me by a man who literally lives in a cave. In my own words, my understanding of this teaching is that at one point in ancient history, all beings (not only human) shared a common language. There were no misunderstandings. This was the language of *kototama*, the language of creation and with each utterance we created. Words (and sound) carry great power, and as the expression goes "The pen is mightier than the sword". The Christian Bible begins with the passage "In the beginning was the word and the word was with God, and the word was God." I believe this idea of kototama is the direction that phrase is pointing.

Writing for me lies at the very heart of my spiritual practice. After publishing this collection, I intend to experiment with leading some gatherings I refer to as "Poetry as Practice". I am interested in delving more deeply into the layers of meaning, the *kototama* of poetry and how it can benefit us as individuals and as a collective society. The way I see it, life is poetry and we are all poets. Not all of us (thank goodness) need to write it down or recite it. I like to say "Poetry is no fun without ears to hear."

Over the years writing many of these poems down felt like as much of a need as a want. First and foremost this is the reason for bringing this collection to print. The wisest thing I ever heard Chief Arvol Looking Horse, spiritual leader of the Great Sioux Nation, say was "Some of us have no choice." Ah, sweet choicelessness! Secondly this collection is for those to whom these particular arrangements of symbols and sounds tickle something within in you which you enjoy having tickled or perhaps disturbs a part of you that needs to be disturbed.

I Am a Poet

I am a poet
I write words

Sometimes others read them

Silently
Out loud
To themselves
To others

Sometimes I read them

Silently
Out loud
To my myself
To others

Sometimes I move
Sometimes I'm still

The words don't change

We do

ARE YOU ME

I feel things I cannot describe
but still I try.
They'll take the shape or color of an earlier day
a Technicolor shadow dream coat within a clear bubble
floats up from the deep.

A hike, woods
some nearly forgotten hollow, a river nearby,
closer to my birth.
Not really sure a memory, a dream...

Later another time and place
many feet of soft pure snow,
lunch alone beneath an evergreen,
tall – rocky – mountains
a board on my feet! Endless bowls...

Or a fire in the dark
giant redwoods, many friends
songs and scents, rhythm and poems,
crescent rising between towering trees.

But this?
Is just the cloth my joy is wearing.
This glimpse, this robe of joy, unprompted, unintentional
not to be gripped or grasped,
but to be swum and savored.

First for me came sorrow though
poignant and pain filled
unexplainable, unknowable,
a lonely frightened child so seemingly present.

Sensitivity...
A gift so precious
a capacity to feel – deeply.
40 years and I realized I had learned gratitude,
I don't get to choose *which* feelings to be sensitive to.

Do you feel these floating unintentional shapes of joy
wearing Technicolor shadows of days gone by?

I'm really not even certain anymore this –
us and we,
you and me...

Are you there?

Or...

Are you me?

ONE

"Gnothi seauton"
(Know thyself)

Maxim inscribed at the temple of Delphi

Between the Worlds

She comes

Always the window
Never the door
I lock the door
I hold it open
I close it
I wait for a knock
That never comes

Always the damn window
And it doesn't even matter
Open, closed
Winter, Summer
Even with the blinds down
She comes...

Flitting through
Like a ghost
No choice
No invitation
She comes...

And I love her
And I hate her
And I want her
And I fear her
She comes silently...

A silvery beast
So wild and free
I bathe in her light

I am transformed
From the body that goes "clunk"
The one that hurts
And cries
And dies

To the One
Whom I am at one with
At one with my brothers and sisters
One with the standing ones
At one with the things that crawl and slither
One with the winged ones
At one with the two legged
One with the four legged
At one with all there is

Why would I
Not go there?
Is it that I am so in love
With my humanity
My pain
My flaws
My individuality?

Of course
I cling to that
Like the bone dry brown leaves
Of a scrub oak
Through a long Winter
That fine bristling sound
For a snowy walk
On a blustery winter eve

A counterpoint
To the silvery stillness
That comes through
My window at night

I use the door
She the window
I turn the knob
And walk out stiff legged and sore
To hear those bristling leaves
to see those sights
I think is all there is
How not to...
How not to?

When this...

Is all...

I think...

I know...

I hang in weightless stasis
Between the pendulum's swing
I bask in silvery moon light
Between the worlds go I

What to Look For in Going to Devil's Den

Ripples, things floating by, rocks that rock and rumble,
small stones and sand, a trillion reflections of
light.

Mossy ledges, water carved stone hollows,
speckled spots of sun, last year's leaves,
rich black earth,
peace.

Flowing, falling water, standing stones,
emerald pools, sheltering overhangs,
rings of fire, fair lying
stones.

Four Leggeds, Two Leggeds,
Things that slither,
crawl and swim,
Standing Ones
and Winged
Ones.

Blue skies, clouds, snow and rain, the sun, the moon,
boy scouts, lichen, constellations,
North.

Hidden trails both high and low, slippery
stones and rocks to hop,
bridges, altars and
prayers.

A single shimmering, silvery droplet
just before it falls,

tears of
joy.

Vibrant new green dripping with the quenched thirst of
Spring.

Sheltered shade along the cool path of creation in
Summer.

The fragrant color filled smell of
Fall.

The massive ice jewels of
Winter.

Things that change, and those that don't.

The Devil's Den is below the high mossy ledge, down close, virtually within, the flowing waters of the river, the path of creation. Not too far, but just a little further than you think. You must take the low road, at least at first, later you may learn to climb down from the heights, to reach this place. Take the low road on the south east side follow the river close, up and up along the path of creation alongside emerald pools, rocks sculpted by the meaninglessness of time, small falls of water, listening, always listening. Smelling the good cool air, moss, forest... Feeling and tasting the dark waters that flow. Breathe.

This is a time for you to spy a fair stone, an overhang, a ring of fire, a place to lay your body down after the shivering, shimmering baptism, you may one season choose. There is a time – a precious moment of Golden Light that fills the narrow valley. Lay your still, glistening, body down upon a fair stone where the waters flow around you, in the afternoon moment of Golden Light. I thought I once heard the sound of wings here – man sized wings...

The Devil's Den is a place which may be passed through, upstream, to a small sandy beach with sacred trees to either side. One who was nearly laid low before bending again to reach for The Light. The other Earth Mother, Life Lover caresses rock with roots. There are prayers here, some lost in deep crevasse, others have followed the path down to its source, its beginning, its ending. Look around, not much has changed here, now and again a tree will fall, a rock will crack and always the slow erosion of time. It has been given me to know that we have prayed here in this way for a long, long time. Perhaps you will catch a glimpse, hear an echo, sense the essence of deep, endless forests which once surrounded this place. It is not the things which have changed, however slight or massive, but those that have not, which interest me most.

WRITING

pulling my guts out
through the ragged hole
that opens
they dangle
between my fingers

i hold them
to my face
feeling them
smelling them

are they warm?
slippery, dripping, grey and red?
do they stink?

I fling them
to the page

plop

Authors Note: I so disturbed myself after writing this poem that I felt compelled to write
the next poem *Discipline* as a different perspective on the same topic.

DISCIPLINE

discipline
a blissful gateway
love
I extend my Self
grace
creativity flows

SILENT SKY

[911]

Rising mist falling beams of light
Impossible flying machines subverted for death
Fell too from the sky
In the name of God suicide

Ultimate symbols of money and might
Twin towers fallen a pentagon squared
No more contrails today
A silent sky

No More Lies

There's this thin black border
Between here and everything else
Between here and nothing else
I keep poking holes in it
Seeing how much can get through
Before the whole bottom falls out

Part of me wants that
No filters, no border, no boundary, nothing left
How much? Who knows
Another part wants the brilliant gleaming light
I doubt there is ultimately any difference
As Tara Singh was fond of saying – whichever way...

Do you hear me?
I'm announcing my resignation
From the whole fucking race
I'm out, done poking holes
Searching for some imagined light
I'm joining the Kidney Thieves
My religion?
No more lies

DREAM

Dream? Dreams, you say? Which one?
The one by sun? The one by moon?
The one where we encircle dawn?
I can't tell any more
I dream in the gray stillness before dawn

Fire, drummers, swirling colorful dancers
Somehow seeing my own dark silhouette
Voice quivering, hands shaking
Reciting for the very first time
before a still tall fire, just lit,
Audience rapt, sparks flying toward the blazing,
depthless stars saying...
"Lanterns hang in the night sky
So that your eyes might draw
One more image of love
Upon your silken canvas before sleep."[2]

Soft, white cloth, soaked in cool rose water
Warm desert deep, deep in the summer night
Love in a tent to the soft steady spatter of rain
Laughter of friends sipping mead and smoke close by
Tears that just won't go away outside the circle
Wild chaotic, unstoppable passion of a lover
In an inside out Oreo cookie
Of white and black and white

Climbing a wall, naked outside a sauna
Beneath an impossibly green night sky following a hurricane
To save a bird from pounding itself to death
Trying to escape through an invisible wall of glass

I dream of stillness in the gray before dawn
And no one can explain...

2. With a grateful nod and deep bow to Daniel Ladinsky's interpretation of Hafiz "Lanterns Hang in the Night Sky".

HOW MANY TIMES

How many times
The third at a table for four
Boy girl boy
So handsome
So lonely
So intelligent
So shy
So much to give
No one to take

AGONIZING JOY

there is a door
in my mind
it's been open all along
finally I find myself
willing to step through

everything I thought
was...
sacrifice is not
still faint but overwhelming
joy still the same

there is a definite imminence
to this eminence
the joy not of discovery
but the discovered

so beautiful it is
to stand
look out at the stars
without looking up
darkness... like that

the smell of wood smoke
not this time
but all times
old times
the smell – no matter
that conjures
not discovery
but the discovered

a longing so deep
deeper still
than a thousand lifetimes
of unrequited love
this is my agonizing joy
burning with it

remembered
unremembered...
beyond overwhelming
this eternal presence
I call it sweet
but it's just sorrow
like I'm made for it
this highly tuned
human instrument

tuned to a fine pitch
to keen in sorrow
tears flowing
all for love
love-never-realized

a dream I can
never awaken to

THE AWFUL TRUTH

The awful truth is nothing changes
The distant stars, untouchable
Only burn brighter
The dark night sky grows
Deeper, darker...

Steps slow with the wind at your back
Pain and suffering infinitely more tangible
Inescapable realization
Ultimate power and...
Responsibility
You chose this

Finally you stop
Give up completely
Turn and walk just as slowly
Back into the cold night wind
Eventually arriving at the door
Of a warm dark room

Entering quietly and...
For a moment
Before Illumination, forgetfulness
You're nearly certain
Just out of sight
Across this dark room
You lie comfortably
Asleep and dreaming

TEARS

I cannot separate my tears
Tears held too long
Have run slow and cold
Today they flow hot and free
Intense gratitude beyond definition
Stillness, so near my source

Tears for you, me, others
Pain, joy, fear and sorrow
Sweet sorrow
Which one? Which ones?

Tears that say I am here
I am nowhere else
I am here
Tears that lead me home

REACHING

I find myself reaching beyond
Everything I ever thought was me
Something much greater—vast
Something I suspect is truth

This reaching is the stroke of a brush, a pen, a scalpel
Of genius
It is the reach of a priest, a poet, a politician
The completion of a phrase
A painting
The discovery of electricity, a microchip
The saving of a life
A million lives
The theory of relativity, the miracle cure
The miracle itself

It is the beggar on the street's
Loving gaze into the innocent eyes of a child
Seeing there—himself
As infinite possibility

Beggar, Mother Teresa, Gandhi,
Einstein, Kennedy, Pasteur, Neruda
We are all equals in this place

BELIEF – MY CREED

I am a holy son of God.

I eat and sleep and cry.

I see both worlds.

I kneel beneath
the blood stained cross.

I am certain of no thing.
I believe in certain things.

My belief is my journey
in wonder, my learning, my choice.

I forget – often, in fact
I believe I have forgotten nearly everything.

Scattered shards of memory, light filtered
through blood red, shattered glass.

I believe I cannot forget completely,
no matter how hard I might try.

Thousands of years of illusion,
still... I see... a dim, guttering, light.

The faint echo that remains is far stronger
than anything, I think, I know, or believe.

Divine.
Inevitable.
Eternal.
It is more than enough.

CERTAINTY

I sense it sometimes
Like the faint smell
Of distant flowers
Sweet as can be
Not a decision
Yes or no
Right nor wrong
But quiet happy whole
That time of no need

Not what I thought it would be
A way of getting or giving
But being
Not under nor over
Or even really in between
All combined
Surrounding me in its inevitability
Inviolate eternal

Not what I'll have when I'm finished
When I've learned all there is to earn
Right here and now
At the tip of my tongue
So foreign I barely believe
I dance around it
Perhaps it dances me
I'll give it a word
It's Certainty

No Need

I wondered one morning if anyone cries like me
I cry all the time for mostly...
I don't know why

Words will sometimes lead me up the garden path
To the gate where I stand...
And gaze beyond

This is it right here and now
Gazing through the open door
To where there are no more words

No more joy...
Or pain
Or need
For... for—giveness

One day I know
I will step through
But that garden needs no work

For now...
And for here
I have work

I can only stand here
And weep

EARTH RHYTHM

Massiveness that brings deep tears
Beauty that is so much deeper than skin
What brought me here to do
What I know
What I know not...
What my open September window sings of

Pine pitch burns, sings tells story of
This moment in time that is all time
All of those I've met
All those yet to meet
Here in this 44 year old middle

All the emotion, every moment
Of joy, of pain
I carry in this instant
Like I was made for it
Like, perhaps I made this life for it

This deep, deep keening sorrow
Never does it leave me
No matter how hard I might try
No matter how deep the pain may carve
Never would I choose not to feel it
To live a life of anything less

Perfectly etched
Perfectly framed
Nothing to cure
Nothing more to gain
Learning...
As if that means to leave behind

Monday night
Like every other Monday night
Or not
The quiet singing
The perfect cool September breeze
Even the fly, buzzing for we might never know why

Just sitting here writing slowly, thoughtfully
Having actually *caressed* this keyboard,
with these two finger tips...

Appreciating just what these keys
This arrangement
I have still—not—mastered
Has gifted to me
This ability to arrange myself
Through words
Through time
Into neatly arranged packets
To look at...
Copy...
Rearrange...

ANCIENT MIGHTY TREE

Oh ancient mighty tree,
If only you could breathe
What word might you say
What stories might you tell
I think I hear you Mighty One

Children's laughter
Childish games
Boys in your limbs
Shouting at pretty girls below
Growing up on a farm
Warm sun smell of hay

What stories have you seen unfold
Beneath your limbs?
Whose lives have you held
Amongst your branches your leaves?
How many sunsets?
How many storms?

You draw life slowly from the earth
Leaves unfurl
Turn from green life
To brilliant fall glory blaze
First snowflakes falling quietly on your limbs
Days marching ever by

Storms you have seen
Lightning you have felt
From the top of your highest branches
Through to your very roots

We toil madly through our lives
Striving after wind[3]
You let pass through your branches
Rustling your leaves

You stand serenely at the hilltop
In unearthly quietness

3. Ecclesiastes 4:6 "Better is a handful of quietness than two hands full of toil and a striving after wind."

I

life the tempest on the sea
beneath which I
the boulder
on the sea floor lie

Two

"You must give birth to your images. They are the future waiting to be born. Fear not the strangeness you feel. The future must enter you long before it happens. Just wait for the birth, for the hour of the new clarity."

Rainer Maria Rilke

CAN NOT BE UNDONE

For Marika and James

I fell in love with You again this morning
Stumbled and bumbled
Fell from such a dizzying height
In the true knowledge
I can not be undone
Could not be uncreated

A man spoke of
A woman's artistic renderings of God
I gazed upon Her myself
My ears his words my eyes her hands
My heart my mind their soul
No longer separate

These echoes a childhood memory
Of Golden Light
No longer separate
The power of my imagination loved
And I knew
I could not be undone

GOLDEN LIGHT

Asphalt, the smell of late Summer
Two sturdy posts above the culvert
At the bottom of the valley
Grape vines hang from maples and oaks
At the sides of the road

Beneath what once was the threshing floor
Of the barn part fallen
Beneath loose, dangerous, old stairs
I built a fort
Maybe it only lasted a day
Memory of golden sunlight
Streaming through the cracks

A man spoke of extraordinary works of art today
I listened while he spoke,
Aurally rapt
I watched the paintings she had made, one by one,
Visually rapt
They were, as we say, "abstract"
My memory of golden sunlight is abstract
Everything is abstract...

I considered what it would be like to say out loud
"I have no idea what you're talking about."
But somehow...
I knew exactly what he was talking about
He was talking about my abstract memory
Of golden sunlight
She drew my memory
Of Golden Light
The memory...

My words, his words, her paintings,
Echoes

Echoes of something
I know so deeply
It can never be forgotten

WANT

I. Want to Want

I am walking through neighborhoods
I'd never want to live,
and ones I would.
I am feeling the possibility
of a thousand, thousand lives.
I struggle with the only one I think I have
and know it's not.
I sense the love within those things I think I hate.
I want to photograph the fat lady
sitting lump like on the bench at the bus stop,
capture that beauty.
I want,
not to want,
to know *that* freedom.

II. What I Want

Only this...
This morning silence.
Quiet, beauty, sweetness...
A window to watch the day unfold and rise
from behind these tall mountains so close.
To sit with my beloved in the evenings
Watch these days – this Sun,
lean close and kiss the distant mountains west;
a place to build my altar,
a small island, protected
for a moment, a lifetime by wall
from the complete and utter wildness
that is this place.

What I really hear when I stop and listen is...
Wind blowing open the doors of my heart
blowing from the inside out
blowing away the sounds of money and need outside
alighting upon those around me
like the smile of a child.

III. I Want What I Have

Not anything else
Wanting what I have is Heaven on Earth;
timeless, immortal, to want for nothing,
no need.

"I want what I have." may be a prayer,
may seem an ideal but really,
I believe, it is simply a statement of fact.

It is not a prayer that will be answered when I...
Not a measure of what I have bought.
If a prayer it may be, then one simply of undoing,
letting go, remembering what already is.

WILDMIND

Wildmind is limitlessness
it is seeing every possibility
and choosing...
them all

Wildmind is no sacrifice
it is seeing the impossibility
and choosing...
no need

Wildmind was once defined
as that which lies inside
now I know there is no...
outside

Wildmind is love
that precedes thought
Wildmind is all...
And I see all in you

EFFORTLESSNESS

The Rain falls upon the roof and into my mind
Through two holes in the side of my head
I feel choicelessness arise within me
Spherical drops skate momentarily outside the window
Where in a moment, a moment ago,
The one and same and only eternal moment...
With complete effortlessness, I saw far

Far across this vast landscape
I have come to know so well
I have stood on every hill
Crisscrossed this desert
One step at a time
Weaving and leaving
An intricate beautiful web
Outside and inside and One

For the very first time I realized
The beautiful irony of coming to the desert
To finish writing The Forest
I caught a glimpse in this precious moment...
Red sand top down road trips
Another book
Far down the dotted yellow asphalt years
I saw a return to the forests of my youth
To finish writing The Desert

I really don't know, or care
Why the rain on the roof
So fills my heart with soft, peaceful joy
I am overwhelmed
Water flows just as freely from my eyes

So grateful for the sensitivity
The awareness to sob
With the overwhelming beauty of
The Moment

Effortlessness is Choicelessness

SOUL SEARCHING QUESTIONS

Why is it we are always going on retreat?
I was preparing for a... advance
I was given an instruction about
"Soul searching questions."
I thought... What to search for
The soul
Or the questions?

Wavering like a mirage on a hot Summer day
Just above and beyond my horizon
Searching for the soul itself
Seemed more interesting
The questions had already come easily

Where to look?
The thought before thought was
Heart Thought

A dream come true
Losing control of my carefully planned life
Barely 5 months in to a new relationship
Facing first fatherhood at 46
An unscheduled pregnancy

"There's a war going on
between my head and my heart
I wonder how they grew...
So far apart?"[4]

That's been the soundtrack these days
These days of crisis and creation
Of darkness being brought to light

And I'm grateful, even lying awake at night
I am beginning to return to gratitude
It has put 'Heart Thoughts' on my radar
Shown me the stark contrast
Between those and my head

My head, an endless swirling turmoil
Of wanting
Of choice
Of sickening indecision
In my heart, a knowing choicelessness

Within this contrast
I find I no longer feel a need
To talk about the difference
between "faith" and "belief"

Three qualities of Heart Thought
Immediacy – there *before* I go looking for them
Constancy – never wavering
No one loses

No matter how difficult to believe, even in time,
everyone benefits from the Heart Thought

I sense in my heart the depth of my faith *is* eternal
I find... the eternal and infinite *within* faith

But this soul
Where, oh where is my soul?
And I hear –

Whirling up through the centuries
A Voice saying...
"I cannot stop asking"[5]

4. With a grateful nod and deep bow to Booth and the Bad Angel "Dance of the Bad Angels", and

5. Coleman Barks interpretation of Jalal-adin Rumi's "Who Says Words With My Voice".

The Healing Rain Garden

I am the healing rain Garden.

I am the sun and moon and stars and wind.
I am all the things you love,
even here in your body.

I give you my Son and my Voice
Who holds your hand always and in all ways.
I love you as you must learn to love your brothers here.

You will do great things for Me here.

You cannot remember all things while you stay here
and work for Me in your body, but you will.
This I promise –
you will remember All Things which you Are.

You will know your tears
your beautiful, beautiful tears.
Each one a crystalline container of the whole.
Even here when time prevents you from seeing as One,
these tears contain your duality; your illusion,
your happiness and sorrow, your desire and your
fulfillment.

Weep my Holy Son. Weep for the world you see
for your brothers who, like you, have forgotten my
love. Weep for the rolling hills, for the gentle
rain garden in Spring. Weep for the mountains
who bear silent witness to the chaos you have
tried to substitute for love.

Your tears are the blessing of the world, which
wash and purify and begin anew the Song of Prayer,
that shows you even here My Love is not forgotten.

Trust Them.
Trust This.
Trust Me.

DRIVING HOME WITH JESUS

For our Father who art in Bethany – John Francis Crowley

The gallery owner
Skeptical of my new home town of Crestone
Pack of dogs at his heels said "I don't shake hands"
Told me he was... "post spiritual"
Over the next five years
We developed what I called a "drive by friendship"
I always stopped, every time and over those years
He met friends, brothers, lovers and eventually –
My father
I finally brought Jesus home
From Tres Piedras, the Old Pink Schoolhouse
At the three rocks, the turn off for Taos
He'd been high up on the gymnasium wall
On what looked like a rusty piece of metal
for all those years...
Asking time and time again "How much?"
Always thinking, just a little too much
That day he wasn't, half price actually
The Post Spiritual Man said
"You've been looking at Him for years
everyone does, but I think He's yours,
I'll tell you what..."
I drove away feeling certain
I would do nothing in my life more important
Than befriending the Post Spiritual Man
Than buying Jesus

One day months later
I got two messages
One after another
"I'm on the edge of not knowing" and...

Jesus had been framed
I hadn't even known he had my number
I'd compared him though
The Post Spiritual Man
Working way below the radar to...
The Crestone Guru
Flying high on the white throne
Not knowing how they were both needed
Just knowing they were
Thoughts...
One after another

Then one day, *years* later...
After Jesus had hung around on my *own* wall for a time
I received another quiet message:
 "To have, give all to all."
Dad was in his 90's now
He'd outlived his wife, two sons, his religion...
One might say he was stubborn
I saw unimaginable strength
Still... I didn't *want* to, you see I *love* Jesus
But like the prodigal son
I climbed back in my car with Jesus for that *long* ride
This time all the way Home to the Father

I hung Him in his hospital room
It took courage, banging those nails into the wall
Wondering what the staff would think
Eyes uplifted, Jesus *might* have been the last...
Or the first thing he saw

And I was certain (and I'm not certain of *anything*)
I'd never find anything more important
Than befriending the Post Spiritual Man
Than driving home with Jesus

LAST NIGHT THE POETS GATHERED

[with dream post prelude]

Later that night...

I dreamt I had an appointment with George Bush
I was late and oddly dressed in black leather
and a brown tweed hat.
They wouldn't let my girlfriend in,
something about a passport
(what color passports do the poets have?)
I was excited, my ego all puffed up.
I – had a meeting with George!

And I was me...
Wondering...
what
in the world
I'd say.

Last night the poets gathered

and we talked, waxed poetic about even that.
We'll never run out.
We write poems about poems about poems.

Last night the poets gathered

There were 26 of us
(Yes, Peggy I count too)
Out there in the middle of the endless sea of chamisa
out there on highway 17 the world passed by –
but not much
maybe 30, 40 cars all night.
Saturday night in Moffat Colorado.

Last night the poets gathered

and always the poets want the world to hear
get published
(and we do)
but we all know
they don't read *this* poetry in the white house.

Last night the poets gathered

There was Jersey Joe,
beautiful Francelia Sevin
so delicate and open,
her name my favorite number.

Last night the poets gathered

Art Washburn invoked the ice man,
Ron Wooten-Greene
with words of wisdom
plucked from the mouth of death.
Peggy, poet rancher –
presence as strong as the heartiest wrangler
words as delicate
as a crystalline lattice of ice
in the midday sun.

Last night the poets gathered

Peter Anderson preacher, poet;
priest of the First Church of the Higher Elevations.
Stewart S. Warren just hitchhikin from jail to jail

with words that get right down to it,
touch you in that place,
and leave you wondering...
why, why, why
can't I just remember that?

Last night the poets gathered...

Yours truly,
just a Crow on wheels
cackling away
before the shining eyes,
the dancing tongues
and clapping hands
of those with ears to hear.

A New Poem

For Michaella Mintcheff

I met a new poem the other day
I love how this happens
I'm introduced, there's a story
Someone says something
About a card, wanting more
Making contact, an extra book
Telling me they know *exactly*
Who the second one was for

It's been happening for years
Recently more and more
First Hafiz, then Jalal-adin
Ten years ago Mary Oliver
Then David Whyte, a house we all belong in
Billy Collins, another road trip
Some random Iowa mega mall bookstore
Diane Wakoski left behind by a house guest
Now Michaella Mintcheff, this
Gift of Hunger

In a way I know this new poem
Not at all
In another way, between her cover
Through the filter of my own subjectivity
She has shared sacred truths
Fears, love, laughter, tears, longing...
In ways others who say they know me
Don't

I took these new poems for a long drive
Because, longing for company

One often knows another
From high desert to redwood ocean
And back
Reading aloud to anyone who'd listen
Mostly alone though, hugged by the "blue wind"
At the edge of the Grand Canyon
Savoring the first sip, weeping into my coffee
Morning after morning

Innocently ignorant of meaning
Pointed perhaps by title
Full to overflowing with feeling, emotion
Longing...
Then returning for family-air-ity
A second cup
Reveling in realization, fully awake
Alive with possibility

POETIC NOISE

It's often mistaken for the ever present sixty cycle hum
Of today's existence but it's not
I *know* the silence that is far beyond 'not hearing'
That lays upon your being like a soft, warm Old Friend
The one where you begin to realize
The space between your thoughts
Once realized, it is the Firmament
There deep beneath the airplanes roar, rubber on asphalt,
Even there between sixty hums per second
Owl and Coyote know and only punctuate the stillness
"Listen, listen. Be still." They call
Still, my endless thoughts - noise
I had noticed though, like the sixty first cycle in that second
That my ceaseless thoughts had turned poetic

SPEAKING OF POETRY

For Stewart S. Warren

I awoke this morning before any idea of myself
And realized we have never really spoken of poetry
Of the awakeness and aliveness
That resides in the spaces between the words
How difficult it is to *experience* these pages
On the sidewalk...
In the speeding cars...
At the dining room table...
Poetic genius, you really are my friend

I have never spoken to you in the past
I never will in the future
But now...
Now—in this space between which
Your poetic genius arises, mine
Where you are not "there" and I am not "here"
Now I would speak to you of poetry

THREE

"If you look with the mind of the swirling earth
near Shiprock, you become the land beautiful, and
understand how three crows at the edge of the
highway laughing, become three crows
at the edge of the world laughing."

Joy Harjo from "My House is the Red Earth"

MORNING

Each morning the dunes unfold
Like the rose in morning light
A thread trails each being that passes
Invisible, palpable
They are experienced like tears

Hummingbirds dance their threads
As light floods in
Sounds, sights, smells
Feelings across skin
Tiny electro chemical pathways
In mind—somewhere else...

Baby bunny, bluebirds gentle murmur
The dawn after rain
Intricate tapestry, beings pass
Threads remain
So much life...

Dawns winged symphony
Its cool desert breeze
Dances
Memory tapestry united in minds time
One

MYSTERY OF THE SAND

For Kelly and Arthur

Invisible things in invisible places
Make their presence known

I'm talking about something big
Vast dunes – mountains of sand

I'm talking about something small
Miniscule particle of sand

I'm talking about the Ones Who Know
How to read the lines – the tracks left behind

I'm talking about sand and wind and water
And how neither one minds
(if they were people with different beliefs we'd call it war)

Constant change, collision, erosion
Blowin – old tracks, stories, new lines

The mystery of the sand
Not quantifiable, but I asked...

Are there really more stars in the universe
Than grains of sand in these dunes?

But all I heard in reply
Was the wind in the cottonwood leaves

What I heard were walls of sand
Collapsing into the creek

Particles striking my hammock
Bluebirds murmur, cooing doves

What I heard were owls speaking
To each other through the dark

And morning born, hour old, elk calf at dawn
Standing on ungainly, long, wobbly legs bleating for his mom

What I heard?
The stories told, the ones long buried?

The sometimes stark, harsh, immense beauty?
Seen, unseen, heard, unheard?

Shall always remain for me
The mystery of the sand

Author's Note: I wrote this poem while lying in a hammock between 2 cottonwood
trees on the banks of Sand Creek 7 miles South of my front door in the Great Sand Dunes
National park. Unbeknownst to either of us at the time of this experience, my partner
Kelly was about 1 week pregnant with our son Arthur.

ALL I HAVE TO GIVE

You have not even arrived
Already you are teaching
What is and...
What really isn't

Prophesized this would be the last time
To live, without love
To live, without learning
What is

In the swell of your belly
I am shown a new beauty
So much more
Than my little self

In your eyes I am shown
An effortlessness of care
In your hearts beats
I hear...

All

I have

To give

THE MEANS OF LOVE

Love means giving
until you cannot give any more –
and then giving some more.

Part of me *hates* this idea,
is terrified of it
the part that thinks
what I give I no longer have.

The part which gets,
feels tired,
believes that sacrifice is real.

I have come to know another part,
I have come to hear another voice,
a still and quiet voice.

This voice is telling me
that all I have to give
I have in limitless supply.

This utterly and absolutely unshakable,
unwavering voice tells me
that all I give
is all I have.

LOVE

Love is involuntary
Not out of control
It has no conditions
From his very first day
My son taught me that
Just his glance and I know

Although a book on my
Shelf says it's so
I lovingly disagree
Everything else may be
But love is not a choice
Love is the firmament

As above so below
So East and West
So North and South
So too where all others meet
The seventh direction
Where we are

No matter how we try
Nothing else will suffice
Love is the freedom
That we seek
It is the Source
Of sweetness that flows...

And is never less[6]

Love has no exceptions
No exclusions

No one no-thing
Not deserving not able
To give and receive
Love is why we are here

6. With a grateful nod and deep bow to Coleman Barks rendition of Jalal-adin Rumi "A Cap To Wear in Both Worlds".

No Idea

I had no idea how much space there was
Until it was filled with you
How could I know what my capacity was
Until it became full

Still, this is not All That I Am
Not until I know you
Like I know them
Each and every one of you

And all those others
Who will never read my words
When finally the boundaries of my heart dissolve
Open wide and disappear

When I love you
As I love them
Only then will I know
Who I Am

For Arthur and Kelly

Your first dawn
And already I know a love
I have never known before
Already I know

Neither time nor space
Nor any travail in this world
Will break this bond between us

The trinity of love by morning light
My heart's eyes have seen is certainty
That no one could have ever explained

DAWNING

More beautiful still
Than anything ever arisen
Over eastern peaks

More beautiful still
For what you say
Without saying it
For what your heart
Communicates to mine

More beautiful still
For what
Like sun and cloud and mountain
We have created together
What that communicates

Like what peaks so quickly, so quietly
Over mountains east
Sleeping through brightening sky
At edge of night and day
Too often I think
I do not see your beauty

Using organs extraneous
I know I look in wrong directions
Or mistakenly think I need
Some window to see it
Yet I know it still
Know you
Your beauty
Our beauty

Know love
Eclipses all

CLEAR SKIES AND SHOOTING STARS

For my favorite meteorologist Keno

My 18 month old son and I discussed the weather
The local forecast was for
"Clear skies and shooting stars"
Together we considered the possibility of accumulation
Say... 2 – 4 inches by morning
I told him we'd want to be mindful
Tip toe around the yard
Careful not to squash any solar systems

With an estimated 200 billion stars in our galaxy
At least 500 billion more in the 'local group'
And countless other galaxies in every direction
Stretching further into the universe
Than the largest telescopes can see
There are apparently more than enough stars
To accumulate 2 - 4 inches deep in our yard

Still a quantum leap away from 'eternal' or 'infinite'
I find the idea of that kind of limitlessness comforting
Arthur looked up into the night sky
Telling me I too can just reach out and touch the moon
Fill our salt shaker with stars
Spice for this never before seen moment in time
Imagination... imaging in... What isn't?

CROW'S OUTPOST

Out at the edge of Edgeville there is a place
Protected not by lines on maps
Covenant, rule or designation but
By utter wildness
Desolation for some
Deep abiding silence
Nourishment for others

This is not really a place
Perhaps an idea, nourished by a place
This Crow will *always* live in an outpost
Near the edge of Edgeville
At the boundary between
That which is thought to be known
And that which is inevitably not

Author's Note: My brother Thom imagined the possibility that our Irish family name –
Crowley (they say you can't throw a rock in county Cork without hitting a Crowley),
might have once been spelled Crow-lee and might have referred to an ancestral family
home place, a place where our ancestors might have once "...lived on the lee (leeward)
side of the hill with the crows. Crow's Outpost is my name for our home in the morning
shadow of the Sangre de Cristo Mountains.

OUTLIER

I live on the farthest edge
Of an already crazily remote place
The Outpost at the end of the road
In the community at the end of the road
There is no reason to come here
Except to come here

And my outside is merely a mirror of my inside
Social habits like the crux where the mirrored light
Stands on its head as it passes through the lens of my eyes
On its way to my brain
I don't really feel like I chose this
It feels more like my nature, a need
Deep silence, deeper dark
A long, tall, cool drink
Sustenance

You might wonder why I don't call
This would be my expression of that wonder
You might think me aloof, superior
What a folly when I too succumb to that belief
You might even envy me, the life you perceive
Truth be known, I wouldn't trade it for another

I make sand castles of order out here at my edge
Stack my wood, fold my clothes
Roast my beans and drink my coffee
Know myself, speak the truth
Write it down – my spiritual practice
That's why I don't call

There's a lot you do not know, about envy…
This would be my expression of that wonder
And pain, and nurturing solitude
That sometimes gets mixed up by loneliness
I have 100 friends in this tiny town, I hug and kiss
But few know the way to where I live
Fewer still, do I speak to of my growing pains

You tell your closest friend
I'd tell the world
Regardless, we all need to tell
I have been thinking it might be a good idea
To let someone else in, maybe just one or two,
While I keep trying to tell the rest of the world
I'm a chameleon
Fearless to get on a soapbox and speak truth to the world
Apparently friendless though but for one
I've found a partner, we've taken root
Now we're three
I think she's an outlier too

It's Different in the Desert

For Lorain Fox Davis

It's different in the desert
You don't question rain, its gift
No frowns and umbrella's
Only saturated smiles
Rain leaves no question of its miracle

Cree Blackfeet
Some say she speaks to the thunder beings
Knurled living trunk of a
Grandmother Juniper
"Slow Moving One" She said
Like I'd never realized it before
Fixed to the earth but moving
Thrusting up – branches
Down – roots
Not always slow
Rapidly swaying now in Summer storm

Never so drawn to a place
No question – called
And the whole precious vast valley called back
Yipping and howling
Yes! and Yes! and Yes! coyote agreed

Air infused with sweet Summer sage
The smell of water in the air
The promise of soil moist and pregnant
With strange patient desert fruit
The People The Holy Ones
Have come to this place for a long time
You can sense it, like they never really left

In this moment I knew why this Slow Moving One
Reached to the East
Other branches sacrificed in some long
forgotten drought
Nothing really lost just fallen away
Effortlessly shaping this moment
Delicate strength, patience...
The desert waits a thousand years
For this moment
Thirst quenched

Rings of the Slow Moving Ones
Will speak of this time centuries hence
A veritable sprint in their terms
Explosive growth and movement
A trunk takes another turn
A twist to the right
Circling slowly heavenward...

Only the stone people know this time

The Beloved dances
Slow and swift
Ebbing and flowing
Roiling clouds
Hot blasts, Summer storm wind
Each direction each shift
A miracle caressing carved channels of earth

I take my holy communion here
Three small berries from Grandmother Juniper
The flavor of desert explodes

Bitter and sweet on my tongue
It is MORE than enough
The flavor and smell of sage
Rubbed in my hands my hair
Speak of respect for the gathering clouds
The darkening West wind says...
"I've got work to do"
Fire to rain down in an instant from the sky
A little more rain
"This is My place don't set foot on THAT peak today."

There's no sound of man here
Just me and the Stone People
The Wind People
The crack and infinitely deep rumble of Summer storm
The sweet smell of moisture and GREEN

You too are invited
To join in perfect presence here
Invited to –

Hear...
nothing

To be...
Still

It's different in the desert

GROWING JOY

I feel a growing joy
In little things
Infinite patience
Acceptance of myself—others
Just as we are

I feel a growing joy
In not knowing
Shedding layers that never were
Finding...
Nothing

I feel a growing joy
In not interfering
Just surrender
In doing...
Nothing

I feel a growing joy
And am continually
And eternally amazed
When I let go completely
To find...

Myself

Falling –

Up

Stand in The Light

That's all I can do
Or should I say All
As time, so to speak, passed
Since I first turned toward It

I further realized
There isn't even a choice
I mean...
I became willing to accept
Choicelessness

So beautiful
To just stand here
Nothing else to do

FOUR

"Into eternity, where all is one, there crept a tiny, mad idea, at which the Son of God remembered not to laugh."

A Course in Miracles

MUDDY PUDDLE

Like careful thinking in Summer rain.

Pondering –
the imponderable.

Happiness –
the sheer warm driving joy of it.

Realization –
there's nothing to think about.

God is –
this muddy puddle
I'm standing in.

EPITOME OF INSANITY

To want...
Anything
When one has...
Everything.

Imagine for a moment,
for the duration of this poem if you will
that you do...
have everything.
It may be difficult, but let's begin.

Not just everything in sight, in the world,
in what we think of as "the universe."
Even more than ideas of multiverses
where every possible alternative
to every situation since the big bang or before
play themselves out in ever compounding dimensions.

Although the everything we endeavor to begin to accept
as our own would indeed include all those things – no
not *only* that everything.

Let's go back to basics
words
building blocks of poetry
this poem.
When I say "everything"
I want you to think:
Infinity...
Eternity...
Or my current favorite
Limitlessness...

Septillion...
One, followed by twenty four zeros.
I recently learned that "septillion"...
Is the number of processes
taking place at the subatomic level within our bodies
—each and—every... second!
It was said that this septillion processes taking place
every second within my body may exceed
the number of stars in that universe I mentioned earlier.
[One septillion, two septillion, three septillion four...
five septillion, six septillion, seven septillion... more!]

If there are more things happening within you and I
each and every second
than there are stars in the universe, then
as I like to say...
"It's a mighty wide sky I call inside."
It's a *mighty—wide—sky*... I call inside

These ideas, statistics, numbers,
so called 'scientific facts' are fascinating...
And I propose – helpful;
like sitting on a tiny dock on an infinite ocean
and dipping our little toe in
these ideas provide a leaping off point.

For me, from here
it's *not* such a great leap to see
how I may well be a highly sophisticated part of...
"All that out there."
You know like...
One with it All?

This really changes...
Everything
I mean *real* eternity, infinity
which is not a multiple of any number
that any number of zeros might come close to conveying
this relaxing into if you will...
Limitlessness.

I actually believe this
And you – you may have agreed to join me in this idea
at least for the duration of this poem.
Are you with me?
How many of you are with me?

Okay then...
Where were we?

Ah yes "The epitome of insanity"
To want any one or any number of...
Anythings!

When...

We *are*...

Everything.

FLIES IN AMBER

Time flies
Killing time
Slow time
Fast time
Real time

Writing words
Pulling thoughts
From sleep
Like flies
From rubber cement

Quickly receding
Subconscious
Unconscious
Here they stay

Amber now
Flies in amber

Nothing will Happen

Sorry to disappoint you, as I too felt I had been waiting all my life. I did the math in nineteen seventy five, I was ten. Two thousand twelve. Seventy five, eighty five, ninety five, two thousand five... Plus seven let's see... I'll be forty seven! It seemed so *old* then. But there I was, the adder of years, the thinker inside that seems to be me, nothing much has happened to change that me. Earlier that year I'd been boning up on galactic alignments, harmonic convergences and bactuns... The Mayan period, the thirteenth on their calendar that was ending soon. I'd come to my personal conclusion an epiphanic apocalypse if you will...

Nothing would happen on December twenty first, two thousand twelve.

Apocalypse—the remarkable misconception. I understand though, and sometimes share it too. That undeniable desire to just get some rest, for it all to just be over with. From the Greek origins: **Apo**—"from"; **Kalyptein**—"to cover, conceal". **Apo-kalyp-tein**—"uncover, disclose, reveal." Apocalypse— The drawing aside of the veil.

Nothing will happen on December twenty first, two thousand twelve.

How long is now? Start counting if you like, let me know when now becomes then. The Perfect Harmonic Note of the Music of The Spheres waits not on movement. Not the second hand as clocks spit clicks, not the turn of the page on my calendar, not even on my galaxy hurtling through the universe at a million miles an hour. I have come to realize that it is only my hand, or yours... Grasping The Veil. What *are* we waiting for?

Nothing will happen on December twenty first, two thousand twelve.

Nothing out of the ordinary anyway. Just another extra... ordinary... day. Not even extra really, just another one of the 365, or 144,000 if you prefer the Mayan long count. In fact... it won't even be the first day of Winter. Everywhere... A very small crack in the ice will appear somewhere. Following months of darkness the sun will shine for 24 hours straight... At the South Pole. A child, possibly my own, will take their very first tentative step. A single drop of rain will fall on a parched patch of earth. A flower will bloom in the desert.

Nothing will happen on December twenty first, two thousand twelve.

Tens of thousands of people will have simultaneous orgasms. The tide will come in and go out simultaneously... The sun will rise and set... Simultaneously. One out of four hundred million sperm will reach the egg... Four or five hundred thousand times that day. In a momentary flash of invisible Light, the big bang of conception will occur. Cries will be heard, babies will be born, boys, girls... A first gasp of purple breath will be taken. Without a second thought, in Israel, a Palestinian teenager will hold the door for an elderly Israeli woman leaving a Laundromat...

Nothing will happen on December twenty first, two thousand twelve.

Long before dawn on December twenty first, two thousand twelve. I had correctly predicted the following: That it would be about fifteen degrees five feet to my South. Winter, at least here, would have arrived. That I would most likely appear to be sitting motionless in this easy chair, a warm fire five feet east of my feet. The earth would be spinning eastward at roughly eight hundred miles per hour. Our planet earth would be circling the sun at sixty six thousand miles per hour, give or take. The sun would be traveling through the Milky Way, at about four hundred and eighty three thousand miles per hour. And the Milky Way, drawn toward that Great Attractor... Traveling through cool, four hundred and fifty five degrees below zero, space... Would be sidling along at somewhere in the vicinity of one million, three hundred thousand miles per hour.

Two strangers will pass each other on a sidewalk. One will smile at the other...

Nothing will happen on December twenty first, two thousand twelve.

TRAVEL ADVICE

(To be followed carefully or completely ignored)
For my niece Tammy

Get yourself a cheap, camping hammock
Search for "Secret places in the trees"
Trees spaced *exactly* the correct distance apart
Stroll small town streets (big ones too if you like)
Search for the funkiest coffee shops
The old original ones Starbucks
Has not yet eradicated from existence
Sit and sip
Whatever it is you like to sit and sip
In funky coffee shops
Search for and listen (carefully)
To an album by Utah Phillips and Ani DiFranco
Called "The Past Didn't Go Anywhere"
Lie in the aforementioned hammock
As often as possible
For as long as you can
Buy a new (or better yet used)
Book of poetry from a favorite poet
Eat some dirt (just a little)
Hug a tree
Go for long slow walks
Have a campfire
Look at small town funky coffee shop bulletin boards
Go to some gathering, workshop, musical event
Whatever sounds interesting or fun
On aforementioned bulletin boards
Be courageous, be gentle
(Secret: Those two things are not separate)
Do three new things — every day!
Go for long ambitious hikes

Contact your kind aunt or uncle
You haven't spoken to in years
You'll find a non-judgmental, kind, loving ear
Tell them I said so
Tell them I said the secret handshake is
"Whichever way..."
Follow the advice of good hearted strangers
Take a left,
"Out beyond the power lines,
up that little side road
without a sign..."[7]
Feel _all_ your feelings
Don't try _not_ to (not no)
Get a flat tire, run out of gas...
And discover
There _are_ good people in the world!
Send your uncle a poem
Give a flower to a child,
An old stranger – both
Cry as long and hard and deeply as you can
Laugh for no apparent reason
Write down your dreams
Talk to old friends
Meet new ones
Trust yourself
Breathe deeply and often
Notice that you are
Don't stop!

7. With a grateful nod and a deep bow to Robbie Robertson's song "Rattlebone" from
Contact from the Underworld of Redboy.

LIVIN ON THE STREET

Out here on the street
asphalt, concrete.
Junkies, poets, priests and profit
livin on the street.

A quarter for each hand out
a hundred dollar tree.
What the fuck's the difference
between you and me?

Out here on the street
we're all just tryin to eat.
We've got habits to feed,
while young people bleed
livin on the street.

A smile for each kindness
an answer to each need.
We got dealers and buyers,
true believers and liars
livin on the street.

Author's Note: There are a few blocks in Harlem where, for a time, I was known by many as "Tree Man". It was at once one of the most difficult, *and* rewarding things, I have ever done. For 3 Winters between 2002 and 2004, from Thanksgiving day to Christmas Eve, I lived 24/7 on the sidewalk at the corner of 116th and Lennox Ave—selling Christmas trees.

FOLIAGE FISH

Foliage fish flies only in last year's leaves

strangely out of his watery depth
yet never to fly above the ground—
in lush leafy green branch

crunchy earth brown aroma is his domain
never to sip blue air sky—
beyond the branches

Foliage fish flies fastest past fall

Snapshot

[I think we may all be poodles barking behind the thick, silent, tinted windows of a passing Lexus SUV.]

I watched a 400 pound, round black man walk side by side with a beautiful young, lithe woman – into a Kentucky Fried Chicken. He was bowling pin round, without the long neck and black stripe. I imagined a lot of thick gold chains and a Hummer parked in the lot.

I was sitting alone in a Korean Sushi restaurant. The theme song from Saturday Night Fever was oddly playing in the not so background, ever so slightly too loud. "Oh, oh, oh, oh stayin alive, stayin alive..."

The people at the adjoining table at my back were saying; "I think she only watches one soap opera a day now... Is it As the World Turns or Days of our Lives?" the woman inquired of her husband. They went on about this old woman selling a house she had lived in for forty years, a dead husband... They were overweight and old too.

Los Angeles is beautiful, brown and black and almond eyes. More Mexico, Asia and Africa than America. More exotic than Shanghai, Guadalajara and Dar es Salaam combined, because there's the KFC across from a Buick dealer too. There's the Ace Motel, Bentleys, Lamborghini's, palm trees and pollution. I never know what to wear when I travel here in the fall, maybe 90 in November...or a grey wet 40.

I'll miss all this. And I feel it's going—to go. It could be better... Or worse, what do I know? Post apocalyptic, anarchistic, blasted landscape; scrounging out some lost semblance of life with oozing sores and deformed children or... something else? Something unimaginably and far more beautiful than *that* fear and horror.

We might still save ourselves but I doubt it. There's another plan in operation, "God's Default" I'll call it. And it doesn't even take much; just the faint echo, that seemingly dim guttering light that we have not quite yet managed to obliterate from our mind.

THE PINK PLACE

And so...
Thoughts turn to the pink place,
where the lusty smoke captures
the heat of my adolescent behavior,
in that joy flower that I touch every now and then.

A woman is singing to me right now,
she echoes in the chamber of my flesh.
Magenta, she says, turning to my pulse's knocking below.
A moment of hesitation trips over my fingers
stretches across my young, innocent thighs, asking
what am I really doing here?

I came to smell and taste the vibrations that feed your face.
My ass rides the sky while my head is buried
in pillows of a recent dark dream.
I smile back at your wanting,
your heat stricken pain returns
to conscious swelling veins of your presence.

We belong here,
between the flashes of this gigantic love storm,
right now.
Hear that out your window?

The high winds above claim the passion
that I cannot contain in this wet struggle of my deep self.
Further on, I touch the flower for a last time,
while patience rests, something unfolds
from my expanding shoulders—

waiting...

SMALL ACTS OF KINDNESS

I arrived on a Monday morning to find a letter on my desk. In actuality and curiously to me, a *photocopy* of a letter. It had come in an envelope with a stamp on which was pictured an American flag, beneath which were printed the words "Justice" and "FOREVER". The prison chaplain Patricia, who had authored the letter, wrote how she had attempted to phone, but "only got a fax tone". I know of this problem and have attempted to resolve it to no avail. The phone book inexplicably lists not the phone number, but only the fax number for the spiritual organization I work for. In a post script at the end of the photocopy of the letter the prison chaplain also writes "the fax didn't work either". For this, and the fact the letter is a photocopy... I have no explanation

The letter is short, shorter than this poem. In the six short sentences there is a good deal of intriguing information. The distinctly Irish name of an apparently self professed Buddhist inmate. That he "wants study materials". A question as to whether I can *furnish* him such "lessons". Information on prison rules about how any materials must be "new in original wrappers". *And*, despite what I've heard about the astronomical cost of imprisoning people, the short letter also manages to mention "They do not have funds to buy books or studies."

Now *I* know—*you* now know... Much more about this letter and my thoughts about it than you would have likely ever cared to ask: The fax number in the phone book, the fax "not working either", my curiosity at the photocopy, prison rules about new materials and all. Oh, and by the way... Neither I, nor the organization I work for, are Buddhist!

I thought about all of this... What a fine example of The World it was. How for a myriad of ridiculous reasons we so often try and fail to communicate. I also clearly recognized one other thing which made of this anything *but* failure. Patricia, the prison chaplain had gone through considerable effort to perform this... Small act of kindness for an apparently Irish self professed

Buddhist prisoner... And that was all that really mattered about life. How it would behoove us all to live more and fully, life being just one long series of small acts of kindness.

This would have been easy to dismiss—I did not have the books being sought, nor am I Buddhist per se but... I have a number of friends who are.

I Beep at Cows

This is about stepin out... Stepin out of the partially hydrogenated, well vegetable oiled machine of fast food freaks.

Beautiful in their innocent curious cow stupidity, they stop, look up, crane their thick black and white necks and watch me fly by... In my fossil fueled, shiny mechanical beast. What are they thinking in their curious innocent stupid cow minds? What am I? I beep at cows.

Fossil fuel, that's dinosaur bone's ya know. Our streets are paved with them, our foundations stand on them, our cars are fueled by them—dinosaur bones! I beep at cows.

I Once rollerbladed up several hundred marble steps on capitol hill. There was a scandal at the time. Something about cigars and blow jobs in the oval office. Which, by the way, I'm all for. I got to the top there were uniformed authorities, but I was quick and they didn't see THIS coming. I made it one full turn around the capitol building. I was flyin, they were talkin on their radio's. I beep at cows.

The uniformed authorities might have been considering a flying tackle, but it was dark and late and no one else was around. Somehow it seemed they had never encountered a midnight rollerblader on capitol hill. Then finally they stopped me—stammering—"You can't do that!" I hadn't noticed any signs, of course I wasn't looking. I beep at cows.

"You can't play games on capitol hill." Swear to God that was exactly what they said - - radios cracklin. There was that scandal at the time... "Are you serious!?" I replied. "Have you read the newspapers recently." Man, lookin back it's like Clinton was Winnie the Pooh. After Pooh we got what...Darth Vader? And now by golly I think it might be Buckwheat sitting in the oval office. A bunch of little rascals indeed! I beep at cows.

I like to ask unusual questions. Mickey D's, Wal-Mart or a BK broiler it really doesn't matter. Blue and white striped polyester, matching hat, or a dark blue apron, gold plastic name tag; Nelson or Nancy. I can never even figure out the combo's. Supposed to be simple right? #1, #3 with a coke maybe? But I don't like tomato's or soda, I hate pickles and I'd prefer low fat milk. If I wanted to add a freakin desert to that order I'd have said so, never mind two! I beep at cows.

"Welcome to McDonalds. May I take your order please?" A thousand times in Nelson or Nancy's day. But at least they talk to you at Mickey D's. I don't think they make them speak at Wal-Mart. Too risky maybe. I beep at cows.

"What do you recommend?" Asks I the fast food freak. Or maybe "Is there one absolutely useless item in these vast fluorescent aisles that you have NEVER seen one person buy at your register? They stop. "Something under seventy nine cents?" They pretend to see something on the floor... "Maybe a pink one made in China out of plastic?" They shift uncomfortably from one foot to the other... I beep at cows.

The instant is upon us now. Confused, annoyed or both, they look up from the floor, from their LCD touch screen. If I'm lucky—or they are—that's when the whole damned partially hydrogenated, well vegetable oiled machine screeches to a halt for an instant... Nelson or Nancy—"What's my *favorite*?" I beep at cows.

Suddenly, out of the oblivion, the wasteland strip mall, sit com, Chinese rip off designer labeled, snooze bar, failing high school, can't afford to smoke pot, or drink much beer so I'll try crack world of youth in the 21st century... There I am—some weird guy, asking a question no one ever asks. I beep at cows.

Nancy or Nelson might hate me just a little bit at that moment but there's no denying there is actually a human being standing in front of their greasy LCD touch screen. Beneath aromas of French fries, polyester and problems at home she's cute, or he is. I beep at cows.

And now I realize, without really intending it, I have developed this metaphor between minimum wage youth, and stupid curious cows. And I'm sorry about that, I really am. I LIKE cows. That's why I beep at them. They almost always stop, crane their thick black and white curious stupid cow heads to watch me pass by. I really wonder if anything with curiosity like that is so stupid. Do you think they know they're going to be called a #3 with a coke soon? Maybe they just don't care. Maybe they know something we don't.

I beep at cows...

Maybe you can too.

ODE TO THE TURTLE HERDER

Take this journey with me to where the turtles are herded.

If there are herds of turtles, there must be a Shepherd,
don't you think?
Yes, yes a Turtle Herder.
Let's take a journey to the turtle farm,
over there where the turtle herds-hang.
Let's go meet the Turtle Herder.

Maybe it's Yosemite, yes I think this is so.
Beneath where the thundering water falls.
That's where the turtle herds hang.
And across turtle Island the turtle herder herds his herd.

He is an old man, but strong.
His eyes are bright and clear,
there is a gentle/joyful laughter to his eyes.
He *knows* what's going on!
You've got to...
to be a Turtle Herder.

There are big turtles, little turtles, speckled turtles, spotted turtles.
There are purple turtles, pink turtles, laughing turtles, trickster turtles.
Whirling turtles, slow turtles, fast turtles—
hurtling turtles.

Now sheep Shepherd's have smart little dogs, but not
turtle herders, no, no, no
The sparkling/laughing/eyed Turtle Herder he has Zebraunicorni you see.
Several actually, maybe a whole pack of Zebraunicorni.

The Zebraunicorni help keep the herds of turtles in line.

Not that they're really much trouble,
they all just kinda hang around and be kind to each other.
You might catch them one day,
resting on a mossy/shady rock,
or a sunny/grassy knoll,
scratching each other's backs perhaps.

You see all the different size, shaped and colored turtles all
have one thing in common.
The Zebraunicorni and the Turtle Herder too.

They're all smiling.

Can you see it?
A sometimes hurtling herd
of pink and purple,
large and small,
speckled, spotted multitalented,
smiling turtles.

The black/and/white/striped Zebraunicorni
are gleefully circling the herd,
playfully nipping at the turtles heels.
Each Zebraunicorni balancing a—
glowing/flowing/burning flower
on the tip-of-their single—mighty—horn.

The Turtle Herder joyfully follows the herd,
like Noah heading for an Ark big enough for
vast herds of turtles.

The setting sun is at their backs,
they're heading this way.

I "heard"...
they caused some traffic today
passing through our way.

Might have caused some...
delay's.

Well—
I suppose it's time to move along now
Yep...

We're off like a herd of turtles!

ABOUT THE AUTHOR

Matthew Peter Crowley was born the youngest of seven boys in an Irish Catholic family in the small town of Bethany Connecticut. Dropping out of middle school, with perhaps death as one of his greatest teachers (losing his Grandfather at 3, brother at 7 and mother at 14), Matthew, as the expression goes, pulled himself up by his bootstraps, passed a high school equivalency exam and tried a year in community college. Dropping out again to pursue capitalism full time, he traded the adolescent pack of Marlboro reds and leather jacket for the more socially acceptable Cadillac and tie. Eighteen years and a million dollars later and having been duly punished for being a good salesman by being sentenced to management, he spoke a prayer aloud at dawn asking "...to be closer to the earth I love." Forty minutes later he was, by grace, relieved of his duties and laid off by corporate America.

In his own version of the "hero's journey", he road-tripped the next three years travelling the country and making more friends than he ever thought possible. Having successfully squandered his equity in the American Dream (a seemingly necessary part of the journey) and needing to get a job, he eventually landed in the highly unlikely community of Crestone Colorado, which is just east of the middle of nowhere, in the largest high alpine valley in North America. As unlikely as finding employment in this curious community of 1,500 souls was, he leveraged his previous experience, this time for the benefit of the earth, and landed a job. Matthew now serves as Operations Manager for a Japanese based not for profit organization. As it happens, Crestone Colorado is the sacred site representing "earth" for this international, spiritual organization. *What was that prayer?* Matthew highly encourages people *not* to be careful what they pray for.

The author now lives off the grid at the edge of Edgeville in the home that called his name—Crow's Outpost, with his partner Kelly and son Arthur, where he practices fatherhood, partnerhood, writing, photography, and noticing and remembering as much as he can.

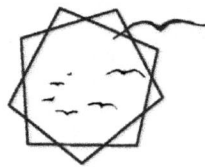